MIGHTY MACHINES

RACE CARS

by Wendy Strobel Dieker

AMICUS | AMICUS INK

tire

spoiler

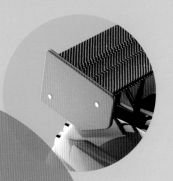

Look for these words and pictures as you read.

engine

window net

The race is starting!
Here come the race cars.

Stock cars race on an oval track. They are built for speed. Zoom!

See the engine?
It is for a Formula 1 car.
It goes behind the driver.

engine

See the tire?

It is smooth.

The tires grip the racetrack.

tire

See the spoiler?
It helps air move
over the car.

spoiler

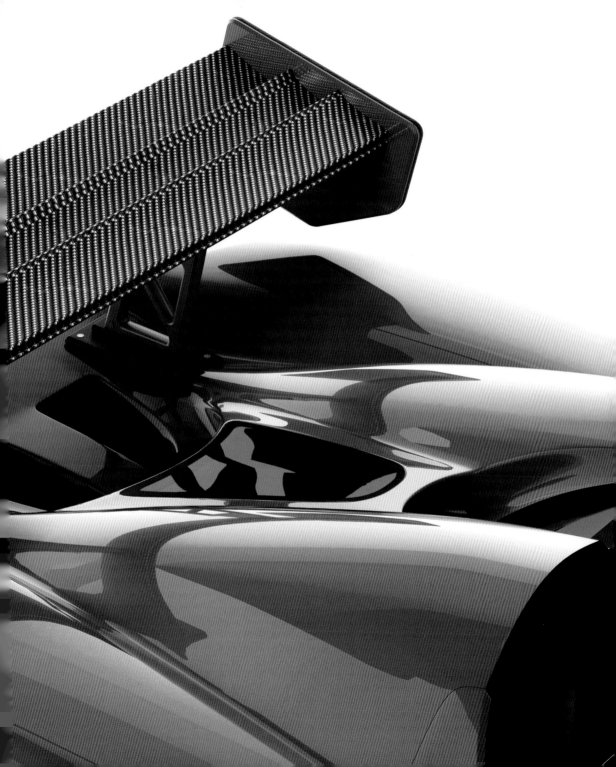

See the window net?
It won't break in a crash.
It keeps the driver safe.

window net

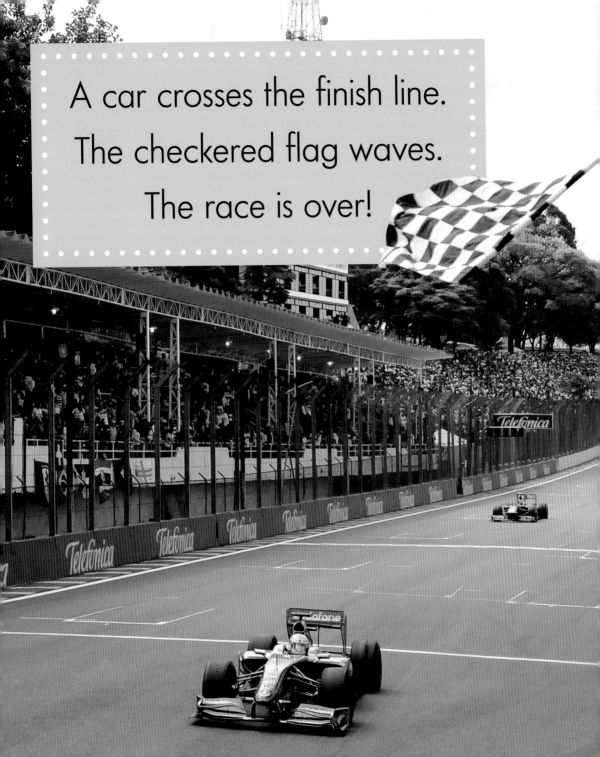

A car crosses the finish line.
The checkered flag waves.
The race is over!

See the tire?
It is smooth.
Tires grip the racetrack.

tire

tire

See the spoiler?
It helps air move
over the car.

spoiler

spoiler

Did you find?

engine

See the engine?
It is for a Formula 1 car.
It goes behind the driver.

engine

window net

See the window net?
It won't break in a crash.
It keeps the driver safe.

window
net

spot

Spot is published by Amicus and Amicus Ink
P.O. Box 1329, Mankato, MN 56002
www.amicuspublishing.us

Library of Congress Cataloging-in-Publication Data
Names: Dieker, Wendy Strobel, author.
Title: Race cars / by Wendy Strobel Dieker.
Description: Mankato, Minnesota : Amicus, [2020] |
Series: Spot. Mighty machines | Audience: K to grade 3.
Identifiers: LCCN 2018024624 (print) | LCCN 2018028773
 (ebook) | ISBN 9781681517292 (ebook) | ISBN
 9781681516479 (library binding) | ISBN 9781681524337
 (pbk.)
Subjects: LCSH: Automobiles, Racing--Juvenile literature.
Classification: LCC TL236 (ebook) | LCC TL236 .D54 2020
 (print) | DDC 629.228/5--dc23
LC record available at https://lccn.loc.gov/2018024624

Printed in China

HC 10 9 8 7 6 5 4 3 2 1
PB 10 9 8 7 6 5 4 3 2 1

Alissa Thielges, editor
Deb Miner, series designer
Aubrey Harper, book designer
Holly Young, photo researcher

Photos by Alamy/CORDON PRESS
cover, 16; ESPN/Scott Clarke cover, 16;
Shutterstock/Action Sports Photography
1; Shutterstock/PHOTOMDP 3; AP/
Russell LaBounty/NKP 4–5; iStock/
photostio 6–7; Shutterstock/Ivan Garcia
8–9; Shutterstock/cigdem 10–11; iStock/
nycshooter 12–13; Getty/VANDERLEI
ALMEIDA/AFP 14–15

RACE CARS